Little People, BIG DREAMS™
NELSON MANDELA

Written by
Maria Isabel Sánchez Vegara

Illustrated by
Alison Hawkins

Frances Lincoln
Children's Books

There once lived a little boy in South Africa whose name sounded like a song: Rolihlahla. It meant "troublemaker" in Xhosa, his language. He was a member of a clan who had lived in that land long before the country even existed.

His great-grandfather was the clan's king and his father, its chief. No one in his family had had a formal education before. On the first day of class, his teacher gave each of the students an English name, and from then on, Rolihlahla was known as Nelson.

Nelson was twelve when his father passed, but he inherited his sense of fairness. It was decided that he would be taken to the Great Place and entrusted to the chief's family, who treated him like a son and continued his education.

Listening to the tales told by the oldest visitors at the palace, Nelson discovered his love of African history.

He also learned that his country had been taken over by white men. They made laws and took decisions for all of its inhabitants.

Big homes, good schools, fair pay... White people had everything they hoped for, while everyone else was forced to give up their dreams! Nelson knew that wasn't fair, so he went to college, wanting to do his best to change it.

When he found out that his family was arranging his marriage, Nelson ran away to Dark City, a neighborhood in Johannesburg.

It was so dark that, at night, there was just the moon to give him light while he studied.

Nelson had joined a group that worked for equal rights when the government set up an even more unfair system called apartheid. Its racist laws separated people because of their skin color, burying their hopes for a better future.

Still, Nelson refused to give up! After being arrested many times for organizing protests against apartheid laws, he had no other choice but to go into hiding. For a long time, he only went out dressed in a disguise.

One day, he and seven of his friends were accused of trying to overthrow the racist government. He was sent to jail for 27 long years. Still, from his cell, he kept dreaming of a country where all people were treated equally.

During the years behind bars, he didn't just earn the respect of his guards; he became a symbol of the struggle for justice. All around the world, there were calls to free Nelson from jail and end apartheid.

Nelson was a 72-year-old grandfather when the president of South Africa visited him and decided to release him.

They both agreed to work as a team to change the laws and build a fairer country. And they won a Nobel Peace Prize for it!

Millions of people who had never had the chance to vote before chose Nelson to be the first Black president of South Africa.

It was a huge step towards a Rainbow Nation, where people of all races would live together peacefully and everyone would count.

And by facing every struggle in his long walk to freedom with hope and determination, little Nelson learned that the greatest glory is rising every time we fall.

Because a winner is just a dreamer who never gives up.

NELSON MANDELA

(Born 1918 – Died 2013)

1937

1950

Rolihlahla Mandela was born on 18th July 1918 in Mvezo, a village in South Africa. As a child, he was given the English name Nelson, and was inspired by stories of his ancestors' resistance against the colonization of South Africa. After discovering that his family were arranging his marriage, Nelson ran away to Johannesburg, where he began studying law. There he joined a political party, the African National Congress, who were seeking the end of apartheid—an unfair government system that separated people based on the color of their skin, and allowed only white people to live freely. Nelson was arrested many times for protesting against apartheid and often went into hiding. In 1962, he was accused of trying to overthrow the government, and in 1964, he was sentenced to life imprisonment.

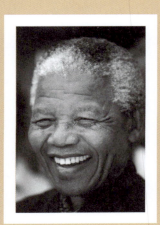

1987   1994

During his time in prison, Nelson became a symbol of the anti-apartheid movement, and people across the world called for his freedom. Upon his release in 1990, he worked with President FW de Klerk to build a fairer country. Together, they won the Nobel Peace Prize in 1993 for peacefully ending apartheid and laying the foundations for democracy. The following year, Nelson was elected as the first Black President of South Africa and led until 1999. After retiring from politics, Nelson spent the rest of his life working with charities and spending time with his family. He is regarded in South Africa as the "Father of the Nation," and is known as "Tata Madiba," his Thembu clan name. Nelson's devotion to justice is a reminder that the journey to equality may be long, but it is one we must never give up on.

Want to find out more about **Nelson Mandela?**

Have a read of these great books:

Long Walk to Freedom by Nelson Mandela and Chris van Wyk

The Story of Nelson Mandela by Floyd Stokes

Brimming with creative inspiration, how-to projects, and useful information to enrich your everyday life, Quarto Knows is a favourite destination for those pursuing their interests and passions. Visit our site and dig deeper with our books into your area of interest: Quarto Creates, Quarto Cooks, Quarto Homes, Quarto Lives, Quarto Drives, Quarto Explores, Quarto Gifts, or Quarto Kids.

Text © 2021 Maria Isabel Sánchez Vegara. Illustrations © 2021 Alison Hawkins.

Original concept of the series by Maria Isabel Sánchez Vegara, published by Alba Editorial, s.l.u

Little People Big Dreams and Pequeña&Grande are registered trademarks of Alba Editorial, s.l.u. for books, printed publications, e-books and audiobooks. Produced under licence from Alba Editorial, s.l.u.

First Published in the USA in 2021 by Frances Lincoln Children's Books, an imprint of The Quarto Group.

Quarto Boston North Shore, 100 Cummings Center, Suite 265D, Beverly, MA 01915, USA

Tel: +1 978-282-9590, Fax: +1 978-283-2742 www.QuartoKnows.com

All rights reserved.

This book is not authorised, licensed or approved by the estate of Nelson Mandela.

Any faults are the publisher's who will be happy to rectify for future printings.

A catalogue record for this book is available from the British Library.

ISBN 978-0-7112-5791-7

Set in Futura BT.

Published by Katie Cotton • Designed by Sasha Moxon

Edited by Lucy Menzies • Production by Nikki Ingram

Editorial Assistance from Rachel Robinson

Manufactured in Guangdong, China CC102021

1 3 5 7 9 8 6 4 2

Photographic acknowledgements (pages 28-29, from left to right): 1. Mandela, taken in Umtata in 1937 Nelson Rolihlahla Mandela (1918-2013) South African anti-apartheid revolutionary and political leader, President of South Africa from 1994 to 1999 © GL Archive via Alamy Images 2. South Africa – January 01: Mandela becomes national president of the ANC Youth League in South Africa © API via Getty Images 3. Thousands of protestors march for the release of anti-apartheid activist, Nelson Mandela, Johannesburg, South Africa, circa 1987 © Gallo Images via Getty Images 4. Nelson Mandela appears at an African National Congress (ANC) campaign rally the month before the first democratic elections in South Africa © Brooks Kraft via Getty Images

Collect the *Little People*, **BIG DREAMS**™ series:

FRIDA KAHLO

COCO CHANEL

MAYA ANGELOU

AMELIA EARHART

AGATHA CHRISTIE

MARIE CURIE

ROSA PARKS

AUDREY HEPBURN

EMMELINE PANKHURST

ELLA FITZGERALD

ADA LOVELACE

JANE AUSTEN

GEORGIA O'KEEFFE

HARRIET TUBMAN

ANNE FRANK

MOTHER TERESA

JOSEPHINE BAKER

L. M. MONTGOMERY

JANE GOODALL

SIMONE DE BEAUVOIR

MUHAMMAD ALI

STEPHEN HAWKING

MARIA MONTESSORI

VIVIENNE WESTWOOD

MAHATMA GANDHI
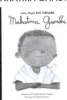

DAVID BOWIE

WILMA RUDOLPH

DOLLY PARTON

BRUCE LEE

RUDOLF NUREYEV

ZAHA HADID

MARY SHELLEY

MARTIN LUTHER KING JR.

DAVID ATTENBOROUGH

ASTRID LINDGREN

EVONNE GOOLAGONG

BOB DYLAN

ALAN TURING

BILLIE JEAN KING

GRETA THUNBERG

JESSE OWENS

JEAN-MICHEL BASQUIAT

ARETHA FRANKLIN
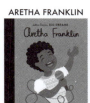

CORAZON AQUINO

PELÉ

ERNEST SHACKLETON

STEVE JOBS

AYRTON SENNA

LOUISE BOURGEOIS

ELTON JOHN

JOHN LENNON

PRINCE

CHARLES DARWIN

CAPTAIN TOM MOORE

HANS CHRISTIAN ANDERSEN

STEVIE WONDER
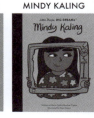

MEGAN RAPINOE

MARY ANNING

MALALA YOUSAFZAI

ANDY WARHOL

RUPAUL
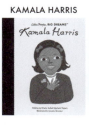

MICHELLE OBAMA

MINDY KALING
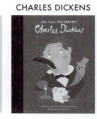

IRIS APFEL

ROSALIND FRANKLIN
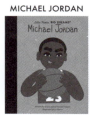

RUTH BADER GINSBURG

MARILYN MONROE

KAMALA HARRIS
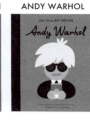

ALBERT EINSTEIN

CHARLES DICKENS

YOKO ONO
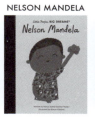

MICHAEL JORDAN
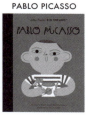

NELSON MANDELA

PABLO PICASSO

ACTIVITY BOOKS

STICKER ACTIVITY BOOK

COLORING BOOK

LITTLE ME, BIG DREAMS JOURNAL

Discover more about the series at www.littlepeoplebigdreams.com